theBASICS
HOT TUBS and SPAS

An Owner's Guide

to Hot Tubs and Spas

By:

Richard Anthony

Copyright © 2018 Richard Anthony
All rights reserved.

— TABLE OF CONTENTS —

LOCATION and PLACEMENT 5
    1:1 OUTDOOR 6
    1:2 INDOOR 6
    1:3 FOUNDATION 7
WATER CHEMISTRY 8
    2:1 SANITIZERS 9
    2:2 ACIDS and BASES 18
    2:3 CALCIUM HARDNESS 26
    2:4 METALS 27
    2:5 TEST RESULTS and TREATMENT PLANS 29
    2:6 ADDING CHEMICALS 37
    2:7 DISCOLORED WATER, ALGAE, and STAINS 38
    2:8 CLARIFIERS 41
    2:9 WATER CHANGES 42
SPA SIZE and WATER VOLUME 43
CONTROL PANEL and EQUIPMENT 45
    4:1 PUMPS 46
    4:2 HEATERS 47
    4:3 AIR BLOWERS 47
    4:4 ERROR CODES 47
FILTERS 49
SHELL, INSULATION, and COVER 51

- 6:1 SPA SHELL 51
- 6:2 JETS 51
- 6:3 AIR INJECTORS 52
- 6:4 DRAINS 53
- 6:5 INSULATION 53
- 6:6 COVERS and LIFTS 54

IN-LINE UNITS 55
- 7:1 UV LIGHT STERILIZERS 55
- 7:2 OZONATORS 57

MAINTENANCE and ACCESSORIES 58
- 8:1 MAINTANENCE 58
- 8:2 SCENTS and ACCESSORIES 59
- 8:3 PLUMBING, FITTINGS, and PARTS 60

LEAK DETECTION 63

OPENING and CLOSING 65
- 10:1 SPA OPENING 65
- 10:2 SPA CLOSING 66

—CHAPTER ONE—

LOCATION and PLACEMENT

Want to immerse yourself in warm water and enjoy a hydrotherapy massage? Hot tubs and spas are becoming a more and more popular treatment for muscle aches and pains caused by long, hard days at work. But before you shop around and choose the perfect model, you might want to consider three major questions first:

Is the floor or ground stable enough to support the weight of a FILLED spa?

Keep in mind that each gallon of water equals eight pounds. Find out how many gallons the spa will hold and multiply that number by eight then add the weight of the dry spa for a total weight.

Will the spa be outdoor or indoor?

This will be important to know for chemical choices as some release more fumes than others.

Do you have the right electrical access?

Most spas are wired for 220V. Some smaller models can plug in at 110V.

1:1 OUTDOOR

Outside, you have the choice to use bromine or chlorine for your sanitizer without the need to worry about chemical fumes. However, the spa is exposed to the elements and can lose a lot of heat in the winter time when the cover is off.

1:2 INDOOR

Bromine is a highly recommended sanitizer for an indoor spa since it has less of a smell. If you want to use chlorine, do NOT use any form with cyanuric acid (CYA) since it emits fumes. Make sure the room is well ventilated; spas release a lot of moisture when the cover is off.

1:3 FOUNDATION

Make sure to provide a strong, level foundation that can support the weight of your spa; use a concrete slab or 'Spa Pads' on bare soil. Remember, each gallon of water equals eight pounds.

—CHAPTER TWO—

WATER CHEMISTRY

Clear water does NOT mean that your water is *healthy*. Every time it rains, pH and alkalinity go down naturally, creating acidic water. Although your water will look beautiful in this condition, since it is unsuitable for algae and bacteria to grow, it is NOT good to bathe in. Acidic water can irritate cuts and scrapes and cause skin rashes, especially on children. Rashes usually start under the arms and behind the knees. Low pH and alkalinity can corrode pump shafts and heaters and make filter parts brittle. In the end, the money saved after not buying chemicals would only be spent later to replace damaged spa components caused by bad water chemistry.

In warm water (above 85°) algae and bacteria can grow and reproduce much faster, so it is important to properly sanitize your spa.

2:1 SANITIZERS

A. BROMINE: Ideal Range (3.0 – 5.0ppm)

Bromine is the most popular sanitizer for spas and hot tubs. In small volumes of water, contaminants build up fast and, unlike chlorine, when bromine binds with contaminants like hair and skin products, urine, or fecal matter it remains more than 80% active.

Pros- Remains active even when combined with contaminants. Less odor.

Cons- More expensive than chlorine.

Common Forms of Bromine:

1. *Bromochloro-5, 5-Dimethylhydantoin-* Tablet

2. *Sodium Bromide-* Granular

What is SHOCK?

Shock is not a chemical, it is a process. 'Shocking' a spa simply means to super-brominate/chlorinate the water to 10ppm or higher using granular or liquid form. You can also use a non-chlorine oxidizer to shock the water. This will not add any chlorine or bromine; it simply helps to 'burn off' any contaminants. Ideally, a spa should be shocked once a week with high bather loads. Otherwise, shock *at least* twice a month to prevent algae or bacterial blooms. It is best to shock at night when the sun goes down and after everyone is done bathing.

B. CHLORINE: Ideal Range (1.5 – 3.0ppm)

Pros- Less expensive than bromine.

Cons- Chlorine becomes inactive when combined with contaminants.

Common Forms of Chlorine:

1. *Calcium Hypochlorite-* Granular or Tablet/Caplet

2. *Sodium Hypochlorite-* Liquid

3. *Dichloro-s-triazinetrione-* Granular (Note: CONTAINS CYANURIC ACID)

4. *Trichloro-s-triazinetrione-* Granular or Tablet (Note: CONTAINS CYANURIC ACID)

What is the difference between FREE (FC), COMBINED (CC), and TOTAL (TC) chlorine?

Free Chlorine tells us how much chlorine is available for sanitization. Out of the three types, FC is the most important since it is the only chlorine in the water that is active and available to sanitize. Combined Chlorine, also known as chloramine, measures unavailable chlorine that is combined with ammonia and/or nitrogen. Total Chlorine simply tells us the sum of how much chlorine is in the water, available or not.

$FC + CC = TC$ or $TC - CC = FC$ or $TC - FC = CC$

If your water test results show a *high* Total Chlorine reading but *low* Free Chlorine, this means that there is Combined Chlorine. When CC or chloramine is present it is sometimes called a chlorine 'lock'.

What is a chlorine 'lock'?

There are a few ways chlorine can be considered locked. The most common example of a chlorine 'lock' is when chlorine binds to contaminants introduced to the water like hair and skin products, perspiration, urine, and fecal matter. A chlorine/ammonia bond produces chloramines which are inactive, resulting in ineffective sanitization. Chloramines give off a powerful or bitter chlorine odor. So, if your spa smells like chlorine, but the Free Chlorine reading is at zero and Total Chlorine reads high, this means that Combined Chlorine or chloramines are present and there is no available chlorine to sanitize the water.

Some people consider a constant demand for chlorine a 'lock' as well. When you shock a spa with algae or bacteria present, the chlorine will be used up as it sanitizes the water, resulting in a drastic drop in both Total and Free Chlorine. This should only be temporary. After a routine shock treatment, if the FC and TC level drop down to zero within a twelve hour period, another shock treatment of the same amount is needed. It is important to overwhelm the algae and bacteria with enough sanitizer. If your spa size requires five tablespoons of shock, use all five tablespoons in one treatment. Do not spread out the treatment into increments of one or two at a time.

Acidic water can also create a constant demand for chlorine. When pH and Total Alkalinity are too low, chlorine is much less effective and can break down much faster than normal.

Lastly, if the Cyanuric Acid (Stabilizer) is too high, Free Chlorine, if present, may be completely ineffective. *See section 1:2 for information on Cyanuric Acid*

How do I break a chlorine 'lock'?

If your water chemistry is balanced (other than Free and Total Chlorine) and you are battling algae or bacteria, multiple shock treatments may be necessary until a stable chlorine reading is acquired.

A chlorine/ammonia bond or Combined Chlorine, however, needs a little more help. Ammonia is considered a nitrogenous compound, and non-chlorine shock can effectively oxidize these compounds that accumulate in the water, breaking stubborn 'locks'.

What are the benefits of using non-chlorine shock?

Non-chlorine shock is an oxidizer which burns away organic matter. It has no effect on pH and will not add any calcium or cyanuric acid to the water. Without fading swim suits certain forms, like *potassium peroxymonosulphate,* can break apart combined chlorine molecules for reactivation.

Common Form of Non-Chlorine Oxidizers:

1. *Potassium Peroxymonosulphate* (also known as MPS, *potassium monopersulphate* or *potassium caroate)-* Granular

How do I remove chlorine if it's too high?

Besides draining some spa water and refilling with fresh water, sunlight breaks chlorine down naturally. For an immediate reduction of chlorine use a chlorine neutralizer *(Sodium Thiosulphate).*

C. MINERALS w/ Bromine or Chlorine: Ideal Range (0.5ppm – 1.5ppm)

Kill bacteria using minerals like *copper, zinc,* or *silver chloride.* Silver is one of the best algaecides and antibacterial minerals on the market. With any mineral system, you can keep your sanitizer levels lower than normal. An oxidizer, like non-chlorine shock, must be used to burn off excess organic waste.

D. BIGUANIDE (Chlorine/Bromine-free): Ideal Range (30 – 50ppm)

What is biguanide?

Polyhexamethylene Biguanide (PHMB), more commonly known as the brand names *Baquacil*, *Soft Swim*, *Revacil*, *Splashes*, and *Aqua Silk*, is considered a non-halogen sanitizer which kills algae and bacteria but does not oxidize organic waste. PHMB then coats the dead particles with a thick gel, causing them to fall to the spa floor for vacuuming. Hydrogen Peroxide is then used as an 'oxidizer' or shock treatment in the biguanide system for complete sanitation.

How do I convert from chlorine to biguanide and vice versa?

Drain the spa; clean the shell; replace the filter; then refill the spa with fresh water. If bromine or chlorine reacts with biguanide the water will turn green or brown.

What are the benefits of using biguanide?

Besides the fact that there is no bromine/chlorine smell, biguanide does not degrade in sunlight like chlorine and it usually lasts longer. Also, it does not fade swim suits.

What are the disadvantages to using biguanide?

Biguanide products tend to clog up filters faster than chlorine or bromine. Clogged filters with high pressure can stress the pump and motor.

Do I have to balance my chemicals if I use biguanide?

YES. Alkalinity, pH, and calcium hardness should be kept in range for healthy water chemistry.

What kind of chemicals can be used with biguanide?

It is important to let your pool and spa retailer know that you use biguanide products so that you don't accidently buy chemicals that should *only* be used with bromine/chlorine. Certain algaecides, clarifiers, filter cleaners, and mineral removers are made specifically to treat spas using biguanide. However, products like alkalinity, pH, and calcium hardness are not sanitizer specific and can be used in biguanide, chlorine, or bromine-based spas.

2:2 ACIDS and BASES

A. TOTAL ALKALINITY: Ideal Range (80 - 120ppm)

What is Total Alkalinity?

Alkalinity measures water's ability to resist pH fluctuation. Because of its ability to neutralize acids it is considered a water buffer and is referred to as carbonate hardness (KH) in the aquarium world. Alkalinity is the foundation chemical of water. If you were building a house and the foundation measurements were slightly off, but the rest of the home—the first, second, and third floor— was assembled perfectly, the integrity of the entire house is at risk since the top three floors rest upon an unstable foundation.

Alkalinity is a pH stabilizer and prevents pH drift. Because of this relationship always adjust alkalinity *before* pH.

Bromine/Chlorine is most effective when alkalinity and pH are balanced.

Is alkalinity powder the same as baking soda?

Yes and no. Chemically, both alkalinity powder and baking soda are *sodium bicarbonate*. But baking soda is a finer powder or finer grade of bicarbonate and dissolves in the water much faster than alkalinity powder when acids are introduced. This means that baking soda does not maintain your alkalinity as long as total alkalinity powder that you can buy from a pool store. Baking soda can also give faulty test results. After testing water for the past twenty years, I noticed that when people use baking soda in their spa the color of the test chemicals turns a very different color than what they should.

What if Total Alkalinity is low?

When the alkalinity gets low it can allow the pH to crash since it is a pH stabilizer. Low alkalinity can corrode heaters, pump shafts, and o'rings.

If alkalinity and pH both drop too low, acidic water can cause rashes and skin burns. The water usually has a bitter or sour taste in this condition.

Increase alkalinity with *Sodium Bicarbonate* (Total Alkalinity Increaser)

What natural elements cause Total Alkalinity to drop?

Rain water.

What if Total Alkalinity is high?

High alkalinity or 'basic' water means that there is an excess of bicarbonates. It usually results in cloudy water. This can cause stains and scaling on the spa shell and in the filtration system. It can also leave the skin feeling rough.

Lower alkalinity with *Muriatic Acid*

What natural elements raise Total Alkalinity?

Lime from grass fertilizer or limestone washing in the spa. Any type of carbonate rock exposed to the water.

B. pH: Ideal Range (7.2 - 7.6)

0—(Acidic)—7.0—(Basic)—14

What is pH?

The pH or potential hydrogen scale is used to specify how acidic or basic your water is. A reading of 7.0 is neutral. Water with a pH above neutral is called 'basic' and below neutral is called 'acidic'.

Bromine/chlorine is most effective when alkalinity and pH are balanced.

What if pH is low?

When pH is low the water is acidic. Acidic water inhibits bromine/chlorine's potential to sanitize. Low pH can corrode heaters, pump shafts, and o'rings.

Many clarifiers and flocculants depend on a balanced pH. Some metal removing products require a higher pH to crystalize the metals before flushing them from the filter.

First, make sure total alkalinity is in range. If not, adjust alkalinity first. Then, increase pH with *Sodium Carbonate* (pH Up or pH Increaser)

What natural elements cause pH to drop?

Rain water and carbon dioxide.

What if pH is high?

If the pH is higher than 7.6 use pH Down or pH Decreaser.

What natural elements raise pH?

Lime from grass fertilizer or limestone washing in the spa. Any type of carbonate rock exposed to the water.

C. CYANURIC ACID (Stabilizer/Conditioner):

Ideal Range (30 - 50ppm)

*NOTE: For indoor spas, it is recommended to keep cyanuric acid levels at 0ppm since it emits fumes.

What is Cyanuric Acid (CYA)?

Cyanuric acid or chlorine stabilizer/conditioner prevents chlorine from being broken down by sunlight. It is a chemical additive that is found in trichlor and dichlor chlorine.

What if Cyanuric Acid is low?

On hot and sunny days, Free Chlorine levels will drop drastically. There will be a constant demand for chlorine.

Use dichlor shock until the desired level of cyanuric acid is met. Trichlor slow-dissolving tablets will slowly add cyanuric acid to water.

What if Cyanuric Acid is high?

After a routine shock, chlorine levels will remain too high for comfortable swimming. When CYA gets extremely high, like 100 – 200ppm, chlorine can become completely ineffective at killing algae and bacteria.

The most effective way to reduce stabilizer is to change a portion of your spa water.

There are, however, chemical additives that release bacteria into the water to eat the cyanuric acid. This method is expensive and does not always work. For the bacteria to thrive, the spa must be completely free of chlorine and any residual of algaecides or clarifiers. Turn off any UV light sterilizer or ozonator and maintain a temperature between 80-90° (suitable for a bacteria colony to survive) until the stabilizer reading drops to an acceptable level. Once the desired level is met, shock the spa to kill off the bacteria.

To prevent cyanuric acid levels from getting too high, use trichlor tabs and dichlor shock sparingly.

2:3 CALCIUM HARDNESS: Ideal Range: (200-400ppm) and TDS

What is Calcium Hardness?

Calcium hardness is the measurement of dissolved calcium in the water.

What if Calcium Hardness is low?

Low calcium levels mean soft water. Soft water is corrosive to heaters.

Add *Calcium Chloride* to increase calcium hardness levels.

What if Calcium Hardness is high?

High calcium results in scale formation (calcium deposits). Harder water maintains a more stable pH.

Water Changes are most effective in removing calcium from the spa.

Chelators and sequestrants, which are more commonly used to remove metals, are also available to lower calcium hardness. Products like these can remove calcium by targeting and coating calcium ions to be filtered out.

What are total dissolved solids (TDS)?

TDS is a measurement of all organic and inorganic substances; carbonates, bicarbonates, calcium, magnesium, salts, phosphates, nitrates, nitrites, ammonia, metals, etc.

The only way to decrease TDS is through water changes. Recommended level is <2000ppm.

2:4 METALS

Common Metals found in Spas:

1. *Copper:* Ideal Range (<0.5ppm)

2. *Iron:* Ideal Range (0ppm)

3. *Manganese:* Ideal Range (0ppm)

How did metals get in my spa?

Traces of iron and copper are commonly found in well water. But there are many different ways metals can find their way into your spa. If water chemistry is left unchecked, and alkalinity and calcium levels are low, heaters can corrode and release metal in the water. Potted plants at the corner of a spa can release copper from the fertilizer when it washes in from the rain. Grass fertilizer can do the same. There are also copper-based algaecides that, when overdosed, can foam the water and create greenish brown metal stains. Iron oxide from rusty material close by can actually blow into the spa on windy days.

What are the effects of metals in spas?

In water, metals react with bromine/chlorine and turn color. Typically, copper turns green, iron turns brown, and manganese turns purple. If you shock your spa and the water immediately turns a color, have your pool retainer test for metals. Metals can also leave stubborn stains on the spa shell.

How do I remove metals from my spa?

Chelators and sequestrants are used to extract metals from the water. These are chemical additives to form an insoluble crystal with the metal ion to later be removed by filtration.

A pH of 7.5 or higher is recommended during this process for optimal results. Since most chelators and sequestrants are organic water soluable molecules they are oxidizer sensitive. These products can wear out faster with high chlorine levels present. It is also wise to make sure calcium levels are not too high since chelators and sequestrants may be used up by focusing on calcium before iron and copper ions.

2:5 TEST RESULTS and TREATMENT PLANS

How often should I test my spa water?

Get to know your spa and its chemistry by testing the water every other day for the first week of opening every season. Then, once your spa is clean and balanced, you can test it once or twice a week. If you throw a party and have a high bather load, test it again. I would recommend taking a water sample to your local pool store once a month to get a thorough analysis of your spa water.

Two Common Types of Home Test Kits

1. *Spa Test Strips* are the easiest and most inexpensive. Simply dip a strip into the water for a few seconds then match the color pad to a color chart. If you are color deficient, like me, strips are sometimes difficult to determine the exact value of whatever chemical you are testing.

Purchase strips for whatever sanitizer you choose to use: Bromine or Chlorine.

Make sure strips are not expired. And if the color pad at the end of a strip gets moist, the pad activates and is no longer good to use. If alkalinity is not balanced, the cyanuric acid (stabilizer) pad will not give an accurate reading.

2. *Drop kits* consist of test cylinder/tubes and drops to determine the value of your chemistry. OTO and phenol red are the two most common drops to test for chlorine and pH. It is important to purchase a drop kit that includes a test for Total Alkalinity. I would personally recommend the Taylor brand home test kit. It is probably the most expensive on the market, but I believe it provides the most accurate result.

OTO and phenol red can expire. It is recommended that you replace your testing chemicals every year.

What is DPD?

Less common than strips and drops, DPD is a reagent used to test for Free and Total Chlorine and is considered the most accurate by pool and spa professionals.

I got my water test result back. What do I do first?

There are two main chemicals I always look at first; cyanuric acid and calcium. The reason being is that if either of these chemicals is high, the best way to lower them is to change a portion of the spa with fresh water. There is no reason to add anything else before doing this because if you have to drain water out you are wasting chemicals and money. If your levels of cyanuric acid, and calcium are okay, always start with adjusting the foundation chemical of water: alkalinity.

Now, let's take a closer look at a few sample water test results and develop treatment plans for each.

Sample Water Test Result #1 (Bromine)

Bromine- 8.0ppm

pH- 6.6

Total Alkalinity- 20ppm

Calcium Hardness- 240ppm

Iron- 0ppm

Copper- 0ppm

What do the results for Sample #1 mean?

With bromine levels near 'shock' level at 8.0ppm the water can be uncomfortable to bathe in, causing eye and skin irritation.

Because of low pH and alkalinity the water is very acidic and corrosive.

Recipe for Sample #1

1.) For an immediate reduction of bromine drain a portion of the spa and refill with fresh water. Otherwise, do not add any more bromine until the reading comes down.

2) Raise alkalinity.

—Retest—

3.) Adjust pH if necessary.

Sample Water Test Result #2 (Chlorine)

Free Chlorine- 0ppm

Total Chlorine- 1.2ppm

pH- 6.9

Total Alkalinity- 90ppm

Cyanuric Acid (Stabilizer)- 150ppm

Calcium Hardness- 40ppm

Iron- 0ppm

Copper- 0ppm

What do the results for Sample #2 mean?

Because the free chlorine reading is zero there is no available sanitizer to purify the water.

High cyanuric acid can hinder chlorine's performance.

Since the pH is a bit low the water is also slightly acidic.

Low calcium can corrode the heater.

Recipe for Sample #2

1.) Drain a portion of the spa and refill with fresh water to lower the CYA level.

—Retest—

2.) Raise alkalinity (if needed).

—Retest—

3.) Adjust pH.

4.) Add calcium.

5) Shock or superchlorinate.

—Retest—

6.) If TC is still higher than FC, there is CC present. If FC = 0ppm and TC > 10ppm, use non-chlorine shock until the FC and TC readings stabilize at the same value. If FC = 0ppm and TC < 3.0ppm, use non-stabilized chlorine shock until the FC and TC readings stabilize at the same value.

Sample Water Test Result #3 (Bromine)

Bromine- 0.4ppm

pH- 6.8

Total Alkalinity- 30ppm

Calcium Hardness- 250ppm

Iron- 0.6ppm

Copper- 1.0ppm

What do the results for Sample #3 mean?

A low bromine level without a UV sterilizer or a mineral sanitizing system is unsanitary. Algae and bacteria can become resistant to low bromine.

A low pH and alkalinity level make the water acidic and corrosive.

Iron and copper can react with bromine and cause a discoloration in the spa water. Metals can also cause staining.

Recipe for Sample #3

1.) Raise alkalinity.

—Retest—

2) Adjust pH to 7.5 for metal treatment.

3) Use a chelator or sequestrant to remove iron and copper. Do this before raising bromine levels since bromine can interfere with the process. Because the calcium level is above 200ppm it may require a second dose of metal remover for optimal results.

4) Clean the filter.

—Retest—

5) Readjust pH (if needed)

6) Shock or superbrominate.

2:6 ADDING CHEMICALS

IMPORTANT: Since chemical strength can vary from brand to brand always refer to manufacturer's instructions for dosage and application for all products.

In spas, products like granular bromine/chlorine, alkalinity, pH, and calcium can be broadcast across the spa surface while running the pump(s) on high for optimal circulation. Bromine/chlorine tablets can be used in floating dispensers or placed in the spa skimmer.

Algaecides, clarifiers, and metal removers can be premixed or poured straight into a circulating spa.

2:7 DISCOLORED WATER, ALGAE, and STAINS

NOTE: Since algae needs a lot of sunlight to grow and reproduce, spas rarely have algae blooms due to the fact that they are usually covered when not in use. Algaecides are rarely, if ever, needed in spas.

A. GREEN or YELLOW

Possibilities:

1) Algae caused by low bromine/chlorine or high CYA which can hinder chlorine's performance.

2) Copper/chlorine reaction.

Remedies: Use shock for algae; in chlorine-based spas, make sure CYA level is in acceptable range first. Copper can be removed by a metal chelator.

B. BROWN or BLACK

Possibilities:

1) Algae or algae plaque caused by low bromine/chlorine or high CYA which can hinder chlorine's performance.

2) Iron/chlorine reaction.

Remedies: Use shock for algae; in chlorine-based spas, make sure CYA level is in acceptable range first. Iron can be removed by a metal chelator.

C. CLOUDY

Possibilities:

1) Dead algae.

2) Bacteria bloom due to low bromine/chlorine.

3) Unbalanced water chemistry.

4) Old or dirty filter media.

Remedies: First make sure that the water chemistry is balanced and the filter media is new and clean. If the cloudiness came suddenly and the bromine/chlorine level is low, shock the spa. It is most likely a bacterial bloom. If you recently battled green algae, the cloudiness is dead algae and suspended particles too fine for the filter to catch. Use a clarifier.

D. STAIN and SCALE

Possibilities:

1) High alkalinity

2) High calcium

3) High metals

Remedies: Change a portion of your spa water (most effective), or use muriatic acid to lower alkalinity; a sequestrate/chelator to remove calcium and/or metals. *NOTE: Some spa 'clarifiers' can eliminate trace dissolved metals.* Then use a 'shell cleaner' to clean the spa shell. Once cleaned, a 'SPA gloss' can be applied to the shell for shine and further protection.

2:8 CLARIFIERS

What is Clarifier?

In liquid form, clarifiers are used to help clear up cloudy water by coagulating suspended, dead particles so your filter can catch them. Clarifiers are usually made from petroleum or chitin.

Use a clarifier ONLY when water chemistry is balanced.

2:9 WATER CHANGES

How often should I completely change my spa water?

Every 3-4 months.

— CHAPTER THREE —

SPA SIZE and WATER VOLUME

It is important to known the correct size of your spa and the volume of water it holds. When you take a water sample to your local pool retailer for a water test, they need to know how many gallons to treat in order to suggest chemical quantities according to your results.

Use these formulas to find an approximate volume of your spa (in gallons):

SQUARE or RECTANGLE

$$\frac{\text{Length x Width x Depth}}{1728} \times 2.4 = \text{Gallons}$$

ROUND or MULTI-SIDED

$$\frac{\text{Diameter} \times \text{Diameter} \times \text{Depth}}{1728} \times 2.4 = \text{Gallons}$$

— CHAPTER FOUR —

CONTROL PANEL and EQUIPMENT

If the control panel is the heart of your spa's operating system, your spa pump(s) are the 'horsepower' of filtration. As the pump(s) pull water through filter and push it through heaters and jets, it is extremely important to keep the water moving. With inefficient circulation, pockets of stagnant water can support algae and bacteria growth even with normal levels of bromine/chlorine.

From the control panel, you can change water pressure, temperature, filter cycles, air blowers, stereo (if applicable), and television (if applicable). The digital display makes it easy to navigate.

To access the spa components, including the pump, heater, in-line units, and plumbing remove the service panel.

4:1 PUMPS

A. MAIN

The main pump(s) pulls water through the filter and pushes it out through the jets, creating enough force to provide hydrotherapy. Most spa models offer various speeds which allow you to increase or decrease the force of water. Choose a pump speed at the control panel to set the perfect massage. Main pumps should run 4 – 6 hours every day.

B. CIRCULATION

Some spas have a separate, low-power circulation pump to keep the water in motion. These pumps do not filter water. Certain spas introduce ozone into the spa through circulation pumps.

4:2 HEATERS

Heater housings are typically made of stainless steel which resists scale and rust. However, with unbalanced water chemistry, the heater could build up calcium scale which retards heater efficiency. If alkalinity and pH drop too low, water can become corrosive to all spa equipment.

4:3 AIR BLOWERS

A bubbling sensation can be acquired through air blowers. These units are simply a motor and fan that 'blows' air into the spa, creating water agitation.

4:4 ERROR CODES

If something goes wrong a code should appear on the control panel. Problems such as low flow, a short circuit in sensors, fiber optic light errors, ozonator failure, dangerous high temperature (above 110°), heater malfunction, etc. will be indicated.

— CHAPTER FIVE —

FILTERS

There are two factors that determine how your water looks and feels: *chemistry* and *filtration*. Every spa comes with at least one filter cartridge. Most filters can be accessed through a removable skimmer cover or panel. Cartridge filters vary in size and style; some have threads to screw into a filter opening, others just push on and pull off a fitting; some stand upright, others lay horizontal. You can also find most cartridge filters available with 'microban' which is antibacterial.

NOTE: I highly recommend using an oil absorbing pad in any spa to save your filter from being clogged with lotions and hair and skin products.

How does filtration work?

Large debris is caught in the skimmer basket. Then water is pulled through a pleated cartridge that is capable of filtering down to 10 – 20 microns. Cartridge filters capture fine debris, oils, and dead bacteria and algae.

How do I clean the cartridge?

Remove the cartridge from the skimmer and rinse it with a garden hose. For a more intense cleaning, soak it in an acid wash (a diluted mixture of 1 part muriatic acid to 10 parts water).

How long do cartridges last?

Usually cartridges can last two to three years before they begin to sag or collapse. They can even get too clogged to clean, even after an acid wash.

— CHAPTER SIX —

SHELL, INSULATION, and COVER

6:1 SPA SHELL

Spa shells are the molds that hold water and provide places to sit or lay. Most often made of material such as ABS thermoplastic, fiberglass, polycarbonate, or acrylic, some shells include 'microban' which prevents algae and bacteria from growing on the shell.

To clean and/or protect your spa shell use a 'Spa Gloss' or 'Shell Wax'.

6:2 JETS

Jets are spouts where water returns into the spa. Some jets can cause pulsation; others can adjust by angle and/or force providing hydrotherapy. Most spas also have diverters to direct the water to different zones in the spa. Use these features to customize the perfect massage to help relieve aches and pains, knots, and tension in muscles, ligaments, tendons, and nerves.

Most spas have jets that are interchangeable and allow you to choose different styles if you'd like. *NOTE: Jets are only interchangeable with jets of the same spa manufacturer.*

A. STATIONARY JETS- Manually turn/adjust these jets to choose which direction you want the water to flow.

B. SPINNING JETS- These jets spin by the force of water.

6:3 AIR INJECTORS

Air injectors are simply levers found at the top edge of the spa shell that you can turn to introduce air into the jet streams.

6:4 DRAINS

When the main pumps are turned on, floor drains and the skimmer are both used to pull in high volumes of water. In most spas, water is not filtered through the main drains, only the skimmer which holds the filter cartridge.

6:5 INSULATION

Insulation is equipped with thousands of air pockets to prevent heat from escaping the spa shell and/or cabinet.

A. INSULATED CABINETS- Insulation will trap heat inside the cabinet, preventing it from escaping out the sides.

B. FOAMED SHELLS- Foam-insulated shells are excellent in preventing heat from escaping the spa shell. Some spa models are partially foamed, only covering the shell. When a leak or problem arises, partially foamed spas are easier to service because of instant access to spa plumbing. Heavily foamed spas insulate the shell and the plumbing. When a problem in the plumbing arises, the insulated foam must be removed to address the issue. Once fixed, foam or insulation must be replaced.

6:6 COVERS and LIFTS

To keep heat in and debris out, cover your spa as soon as you are done using it. Most spa covers are manufactured from tapered foam and include a polyethylene vapor barrier. Spa covers are not meant to carry heavy weight. Do not stand or sit on the cover. Brush snow off in the winter time to prevent the cover from developing sag. Use cover locks to prevent children from accessing the spa when unattended.

Hydraulic lifts are a great tool to take the spa cover off and put it back on with ease. They can be installed on most spa models.

— CHAPTER SEVEN —

IN-LINE UNITS

7:1 UV LIGHT STERILIZERS

UV light sterilizers will clear cloudy and green water caused by algae and bacteria. As water passes through the wet chamber of the unit, germicidal lamps emit UV-C light which mutates algae spores, bacteria, viruses, pathogens, and other microorganisms so they cannot reproduce.

As UV light sterilizers prevent algae and bacterial blooms, they help save on bromine/chlorine usage by leaving less microorganisms in the water, reducing the demand for a sanitizer.

Ultraviolet light also breaks down chloramines which cause a chlorine-smelling odor.

Do UV light sterilizers break down bromine and chlorine?

YES. But with normal levels of cyanuric acid, chlorine will remain protected as it passes through the UV sterilizer during circulation. Cyanuric acid does not protect bromine.

Do I need to use bromine or chlorine with a UV light sterilizer?

YES. Although UV light units sterilize 99.9% of the water that runs through it, you still need a sanitizer present in the water. For example, if a virus, parasite, or mold enters the spa water, the only way a UV sterilizer can sanitize it is if it passes through the unit. This is why a residual level of bromine/chlorine is necessary.

How long do UV bulbs last?

Usually 2-3 years before they need to be replaced.

7:2 OZONATORS

Ozonators produce ozone gas that dissolves into the water as it passes through the unit. Ozone works to oxidize organic contaminants, reducing the demand for bromine/chlorine. Ozone is safe and pH neutral therefore it will not affect water chemistry. Like UV sterilizers, ozone destroys bacteria, algae, viruses, and odors. It also breaks down chloramines.

Do I need to use bromine or chlorine with an ozonator?

YES. Although having an ozonator will reduce the demand for sanitizer by 25%, you still need residual levels of bromine/chlorine to fully sanitize the water.

How long do ozonators last?

Unfortunately, ozonators will NOT last the life of your spa. They usually need to be replaced every 2-3 years.

— CHAPTER EIGHT —

MAINTENANCE and ACCESSORIES

8:1 MAINTANENCE

A. DAILY- Skim the surface of the water to remove any leaves, bugs, or other unwanted debris.

B. WEEKLY- Clean the skimmer basket (if applicable). Vacuum. Shock the spa after high bather loads. Rinse off any oil collecting pad(s). Test spa water. Apply chemicals as needed.

C. MONTHLY- Clean or replace the filter. Replace oil collecting pad(s).

Two Common types of Spa Vacuums:

1. *Battery-powered-* Available in different sizes and strengths. These have a reusable filter bag inside which captures the debris you are vacuuming. Some models come with rechargeable batteries. Most types come with their own pole or they can attach to a standard pool vacuum pole.

2. *Siphon-* Requires no power. Simply attach the drain tube to the pump head and submerge it in the water. Allow the drain tube to hang over the spa side down to the floor. Squeeze the siphon until the water starts to flow.

8:2 SCENTS and ACCESSORIES

A. SCENTS

Spa scents provide aromatherapy and are available in various fragrances as liquid or dissolvable solids, like 'SpaBombs'. It is wise to use an oil-absorbing pad when using any kind of spa scent to save your filter from clogging.

B. ACCESSORIES *Ask your pool and spa retailer about spa options.

   1. *Stereos*

   2. *Programmable LED and fiber optic lighting*

   3. *Televisions*

   4. *Waterfalls*

   5. *Steps*

8:3 PLUMBING, FITTINGS, and PARTS

Filtration System: Order of Water flow

SKIMMER BASKET → CARTRIDGE FILTER → PUMP→ UV LIGHT STERILIZER → HEATER→ OZONATOR

A. PIPES and HOSES

   1. *PVC pipe and flexible PVC.* Hard PVC pipes and fittings get permanently connected with glue and primer. Flexible PVC can be secured with glue and primer or with a

male barbed fitting and clamp. Commonly available in ¾", 1", 1¼", 1½", or 2"

2. *Clear hose* can be used on any filtration system. Although they cannot be glued, barbed male adapters with a clamp will work just fine to secure them. Commonly available in ¾", 1", 1¼", 1½" or 2"

B. FITTINGS

NOTE: Wrap Teflon tape around male threaded fittings; then, over the Teflon, apply a small bead of clear silicone around the edge of the threads before connecting. The silicone will create its own gasket as the fitting is twisted in. Silicone is not permanent and can be ripped off when needed. Hand-tighten all threaded fittings. Do not use a wrench.

1. *Unions* are a twist-apart piece used to easily connect/disconnect plumbing; available in various female/male combinations; threaded or PVC glue-in.

2. *Manifolds*- Splits water flow from one large (female 2" PVC) opening to several smaller (male ¾" barbed) openings, feeding water to the jets.

3. *PVC fittings*- glue-in; available in various female/male combinations, elbows, and couplings.

4. *Barbed fittings*- Male insert fittings used with a clamp to secure flexible PVC or clear hose.

C. VALVES

1. *Ball valves* and *knife gates* are designed to provide an easy way to stop the flow of water by turning a knob or pushing down on a handle. Usually available in 1½" to 2"; threaded or glue-in option; various male/female connection options.

— CHAPTER NINE —

LEAK DETECTION

Having a leak and not knowing where it is can be stressful. There are a few things you can do to eliminate some possibilities:

First, check for cracks in the spa shell. Then examine each jet, drain, and light housing. If you find something cracked, most likely, that's where the spa is leaking.

Open the service panel of the spa cabinet and look for obvious leaks first; all the visible plumbing (not hidden beneath foam insulation). If your spa shell and plumbing are heavily foamed, cracked plumbing will be hard to pinpoint. Because of the foam, water will travel through the porosity and drain out at a completely different location than the defective area.

If you can't find the leak contact your local pool and spa professional for service.

— CHAPTER TEN —

OPENING and CLOSING

10:1 SPA OPENING

INSTRUCTIONS

1. Rinse and clean the spa shell then run fresh water into the spa while all drains are open to clear out any residual anti-freeze in the plumbing.

2. Close all drain lines and replace the filter.

3. Fill the spa with a garden hose to operating level.

4. Turn on the power.

5. Make sure all jets are open so pressure doesn't build up and air can escape the lines when the pump is turned on.

6. Release all the trapped air in the lines by running the spa on 'prime' cycle (if applicable). Otherwise, to prime the lines, turn the pump(s) on high for 10 seconds, then turn them off, then back on again to release the air.

7. Test the water and add chemicals to balance.

8. Set the water temperature and cover the spa.

10:2 SPA CLOSING

INSTRUCTIONS

1. Turn off the power.

2. Remove the water from the spa by opening all drains.

3. Drain the pumps, air blower, and heater.

4. Remove the filter(s).

5. Blow out the pipes to make sure ice expansion does not break the lines during freezing temperatures. You can add antifreeze if you'd like.

6. Remove the rest of the water.

7. Clean the spa shell and cover.

8. Secure the cover and lock it.

Other titles in 'theBASICS' series:

SWIMMING POOLS

FRESHWATER AQUARIUMS

SALTWATER AQUARIUMS

Made in the USA
Monee, IL
23 April 2021